AIMING HIGH

Thoughts, Quotes & Phrases
for the "Business of Life"

Aldean T. Pearson

Unless otherwise noted, all scripture is from the *King James Version.*

AIMING HIGH: Thoughts, Quotes & Phrases for the "Business of Life"
By Aldean T. Pearson

© 2022 by Aldean T. Pearson
PO Box 5811 | Takoma Park, MD 20913

ISBN: 979-8-9850160-0-0

Editing by Jordan Media Services | PO Box 161593 | Fort Worth, Texas USA | 76161
jordanmediaservices.com

Cover Design, Typesetting/Layout by Ken Fraser | grafxedge@gmail.com | impactbook-designs.com

Printed in the United States of America

Contents

Acknowledgments

No one climbs a mountain alone. As you climb, many voices are heard of those who have inspired, trained and even chastised you—encouraging you to continue on and never give up. This book is the result of those many voices in my life—voices that have helped me recognize and value my God-given gifts and share them with the world.

My Foundation:

To God and my Lord and Savior, Jesus Christ: Thank You for the gift of words that He has placed inside me. He has allowed me to see my value to achieve in life things I could not have planned.

To my late parents, Gretel and Felix Pearson: You instilled in me a strong spiritual foundation, and an understanding of the provisional nature of God. When I look back on how you cared for my siblings and me with "two fish and five loaves," it gave me the faith and strength to trust God in every area of my life. Thank you for inspiring that legacy in me by your example.

My True Driving Force:

Julianne Pearson: Proverbs 18:22, NIV, says, "He who finds a wife finds what is good and receives favor from the Lord." I am so blessed to have such *good* in my life—one who encourages me through life's challenges, supports me as I establish and pursue my vision and purpose, and listens to my heart and not just my words. I am the MAN I am today because you are the good WOMAN in my life. It is such a blessing in life to have someone who can celebrate with me in triumphs, and pray with me through problems.

Alayna and Aldean II: God has truly blessed me with two talented and gifted children. You have been my inspiration. You have challenged me to reach my full potential in every area of life.

Hopefully, the fruit you have seen will inspire you to know that you can also achieve and grow from your past. I am excited about the fruit that will come forth from your trees.

My Bricks:

James H. Beauter: You took a young college kid and allowed him to grow in areas he could not readily see. Thanks for over six years of mentorship in business, and a friendship that continues today.

Connie Smith-Fields: You saw a young college student with potential, and for over eight years taught and guided me on the right social path of life. Thanks for your counseling chair, firm yet loving words, and your giving heart.

To the many others who tirelessly and selflessly contributed to my life by encouraging, pushing and motivating me, I say thank you for encouraging me along my journey.

Introduction

"Our deepest fear is not that we are inadequate. Our deepest fear is that we are powerful beyond measure. It is our light, not our darkness, that frightens us most...We were born to make manifest the glory of God that is within us. It's not just in some of us; it's in all of us. And when we let our own light shine, we unconsciously give other people permission to do the same. As we are liberated from our own fear, our presence automatically liberates others."

—Marianne Williamson

—∞∞—

After graduating from college in 1992 and getting married in 1994, I quickly learned that life was more than just waking up each morning and attacking the moment. Life no longer just involved my thoughts, actions or motives. I realized real life was achieved by recognizing my value and what I do with and for others.

In 2001, as a self-employed business owner, I got the opportunity to train, lead and develop people both in business and life. I noticed that, as with most people, it was hard for them to stay motivated and energized. Recommending another book to read was not getting the results I desired. That's when I realized I had a knack for creating inspirational quotes and phrases—words that connected with those who heard me speak, train and coach.

In 2008, after much prompting and encouragement from others, I began cataloging those sayings. What now are known as *Al-isms,* these quotes have kept me humble and my head bowed—kept my mind stable and driven me to continue moving onward and upward. It is my hope that as you ponder this collection, they do the same for you—that daily you will read something that will energize your to-day, give hope to your tomorrow, and forever alter your perceptions. Brace yourself for AIMING HIGH!

Al Pearson

Life
Quotes

"He that followeth after righteousness and mercy findeth life, righteousness, and honour."
— Proverbs 21:21

Life Quotes

Without the rough side of the mountain, you would never be able to climb it. Your life experiences have allowed you to continue the climb to reach this point in your life. Enjoy the scenery at this level, but don't settle for it as your final destination. Just imagine who you will become as you continue to climb!

⸻ ⚮ ⸻

Your past is just that—your "past." It's not an indicator of your future, but a preparer for it.

⸻ ⚮ ⸻

Understand the difference between try and train. When you try something, you don't know if you will fail or succeed. When you train for something, you have an expectation of success.

⸻ ⚮ ⸻

You can either change history by what you learn, or repeat it by what you ignore.

⸻ ⚮ ⸻

There are three possible outcomes in pursuit: You will learn; you will achieve; or you will accomplish both. Failure then becomes a mile marker, not an identity.

⸻ ⚮ ⸻

Don't be fooled by the temporary pressures of life. Remember, it is only through and under pressure that diamonds are made.

Champions don't wait for an opportunity to prepare; they prepare for an opportunity. Start preparing today for what you desire tomorrow.

Think above what is ordinary or extraordinary. Then you will discern that the sky is not your limit—it is your floor. You were created to reach far beyond the sky. Therefore, never let success go to your head, and never let failure pierce your heart.

Just as our natural eyes open when we're in dark or lower light, our spiritual eyes (if we allow them) become more acute when going through dark or dim times.

Like a picture, life is sometimes difficult to see with clarity because we are so close up on it. Take a few steps back so you can more accurately assess what's in front of you. You may be surprised at what you see.

Walk today like you've already arrived. Push like you're almost there.

There is danger in delay. Frustration often builds through procrastination and missed opportunities. You deserve better. You are better. You can be better. Start today!

Protection can sometimes be clothed in what feels at the moment like rejection.

⁓

It is always better to live a good name than talk a good game. Your life is your true message.

⁓

Success is not generated by the earthly family you're in, but is truly based on cultivation of the gift within. Continue to build you and your results will follow. NO EXCUSES!

⁓

When you have no vision for your own life, you will continually make everyone else's dreams come true.

⁓

Success is often found at the crossroads of preparation and opportunity.

⁓

Training is an activity that builds growth. Teaching is an opportunity for learning that fosters growth.

⁓

Peace should be your rule of thumb. When you don't have peace about a decision, there is no such thing as a "missed opportunity."

⁓

What you are presently doing is what you envision for your future. The results of what people see you doing is what you've already seen.

"Mistakes prove you're human;
progress proves you're persistent.
Keep fighting!"

It is through the pain of the past that the passion of the present can lead you to the purpose of your future. Therefore, your pain leads you to your passion and your passion helps you find your purpose.

Let your past be used to *refine* you, not *define* you.

Accomplishments are the bricks that are placed on the framework of potential.

You can be a great dreamer; however, without action you can never become a great achiever. Let your efforts follow your dreams.

A winner wins occasionally. A champion wins continually.

Mistakes prove you're human; progress proves you're persistent. Keep fighting!

Every opportunity for your opinion is not always an opportunity for you to share it.

Quality does not need to be announced; it's identified.
Your current position may not be where you maximize your potential, but don't allow it to be a place of frustration. Keep growing YOU and watch the change in you!

Tomorrow is not promised, so make your tomorrow reachable today.

Don't get so caught up in what *isn't* that you miss what *is*!

You cannot make excuses and progress at the same time. Accountability and responsibility promote growth. Excuses lay a foundation for the "Blame Game." Don't sign up for that class.

There is always at least a nugget of reward when you press through what at first seems difficult.

It is better to do something you like and create an income than to do something just to have an income. Love life and never money.

Practice excellence and you'll attract perfection.

Never allow anyone access to foreclose on your dreams. Keep your imagination so strong and alive that you can taste its fruition. Keep believing—that's the power of fulfilled imagination.

The power of a tree isn't in its height but in its roots. Keep driving your roots through personal development and watch your tree stand tall.

Those who appreciate what they learn, teach what they learn. Those who appreciate what they teach learn more.

———⊶⊷———

Although value and purpose are usually the "drivers" of life, passion is the fuel that gets you there.

———⊶⊷———

Always keep your character ahead of your money and your money will have staying power.

———⊶⊷———

Training is the rain that waters the garden of our intentions, beliefs and attitude.

———⊶⊷———

Continue to learn and endure in the process, to earn and enjoy the victory.

———⊶⊷———

Even though it sometimes seems life is at its worst, the sun comes out to remind us of its true power and purpose. The day does get brighter.

———⊶⊷———

Nip negativity in the bud without prejudice, and positivity can grow freely.

———⊶⊷———

Opposition creates opportunity and opportunities are maximized through trust and obedience.

When you're unable to celebrate someone else's success, you limit your own.

———⚬⚬⚬———

When you purify your mind, your mouth gets in line. You are the creator of your future.

———⚬⚬⚬———

A dream without a plan and action can become a nightmare.

———⚬⚬⚬———

Great people see adversity as an opportunity to excel and make a positive impact.

———⚬⚬⚬———

Keep your head up and your thoughts forward.

———⚬⚬⚬———

Progress is not based on comparison to others; it is simply the ability to notice that you improved upon yesterday.

———⚬⚬⚬———

Yesterday's tools may not be adequate for today's repairs. You must understand that you are always learning. The man who thinks he knows it all has death for a friend.

———⚬⚬⚬———

The beauty of a day is not defined by the weather, the friends you're with, or even how you feel; it is defined by the gratitude of the one who is able to see it.

"Great people see adversity as an opportunity to excel and make a positive impact."

Whenever you feel you can't, remember the first part of that word is "can," and stretch your assumed limits until they break.

—⊶⊷⊶—

Your pulse lets me know if you're alive; your fruit lets me know if you're living.

—⊶⊷⊶—

As you climb to the top of each mountain, just know that what you see at the top only represents the apex of that particular level. As you continue to climb, your life will be the light that gives light and hope to those behind whose candles have temporarily dimmed.

—⊶⊷⊶—

Every time we live backward it's always evil.

—⊶⊷⊶—

Limitations are only limited to your imagination. Think BIG. Dream BIG. Live BIGGER!

—⊶⊷⊶—

What may appear to be an "overnight success" to the viewer, is oftentimes a lifetime of work and process for the achiever.

We often make a priority of those things we are passionate about and procrastinate with those things we dislike. Feelings should not be the motivator of our actions; purpose should. Pursue purpose daily and you'll attract the life you were created to live.

Trust in the sovereignty of God rather than the humanity of man.

You can go to school to become certified, or you can live life and become qualified. Some things are best taught through experience.

Oftentimes, we hear the words, "That's life," as a response to challenges we face. While that may be "the situation of the day," it's not "life." Look at life's challenges as a preparation for the next stage of maturation. You were meant to live life abundantly; anything else may be factual, but it's not truthful.

Live your life to be purposeful, not popular. The rewards of a purposeful life far outweigh those of fame.

Like the story of the butterfly emerging from the cocoon, don't expect someone to deliver you from the process. Allow the process to strengthen your wings to fly successfully.

It is said, "You can be anything you want to be, if you just try hard enough." However, you can only be GREAT at the things you are gifted to be. Let your strengths guide your purpose.

The weight of obligation can hinder you from achieving all the greatness that's within you. Do things out of love and not obligation. Release yourself from ALL forms of obligation. That's how you truly become "debt free"!

"Believing in God keeps you talking. Trusting in God gets you walking."

A little rain must fall in your life sometimes for you to see the flowers of a blessing.

—⁓—

Sometimes it takes having to look through the morass of life to find the daily gems that are hidden.

—⁓—

When you find yourself spending more money and time on pleasure rather than purpose, your life eventually becomes frustrating and unbalanced.

—⁓—

Life is less about convincing and converting, and more about educating and evolving.

—⁓—

Believing in God keeps you talking. Trusting in God gets you walking.

—⁓—

Never let fear shape your response to life. Maximize each moment of your day. In it you will find jewels of opportunity.

—⁓—

Success in life is not determined by how you FEEL, but what you FULFILL. Do it until it's DONE!

—⁓—

What you feed your mind will eventually feed your will.

Pursuing purpose requires you to be strong when being weak seems comfortable.

When you ignore your strengths, you'll be embarrassed by your weaknesses. Do what you do well and leverage the rest.

Expect success and refuse to apologize for desiring more. Success often has another level.

Understanding your purpose and the acknowledgement of the call on your life opens the door to its fulfillment. Dream BIG as you walk each day with PURPOSE!

Anything gained illegitimately cannot have legitimate expectations.

If you don't value what you have, then it becomes easy to discard what you hold.

Yesterday is over. Bring today into focus. It's the only way to effectively prepare for better tomorrows.

Dreams and visions are essential to pursuing a productive life. You can never seize what you don't see. What do you see?

Be still! You can hear so much more.

—∞—

The power of growth is found in frequency and in consistency. Take a look at your areas of growth. You will find that the greater the consistency the greater the growth. Find new areas to be consistent and set your frequency, then watch your growth widen.

—∞—

Success starts on the inside, before ever manifesting externally. Internal success gives you the foundational tools necessary to persevere through the temporary roadblocks to fulfill purpose.

—∞—

Talk about your vision and not your view; even though people oftentimes judge you by your view and not your vision.

—∞—

What you physically see is always history.

—∞—

Make your future so bright that it casts a shadow on your past. It doesn't mean your past doesn't exist; it just means it doesn't captivate your attention.

—∞—

The mundane things become important when you list and accomplish them.

When failure is not an option, challenges become just an obstacle and success becomes measurable.

Success is the actualization of a former visualization. See it in order to seize it.

Access to success is only available to those willing to persevere. Refuse to accept failure, and be bold enough to let go!

The benefits of a discipline far outweigh the perfunctory nature of a routine. Stay present and conscious in what you do repeatedly.

The benefit of endurance far outweighs the ease of giving up. *Good* things may come to those who wait, but *great* things come to those who work while they wait. Be determined to be a conqueror.

Haters are an indicator that you are doing something right. Rarely do people shoot arrows down. Awaken to the flip side and pursue ALL of your purpose and potential. Keep looking beyond your haters instead of looking at them.

Keep working with what you have that may seem little or small to others until you break through. Even a match can light a darkened room.

"Success is the actualization of a former visualization. See it in order to seize it."

The beginning of success is caused by pressing through in moments of failure.

A balanced life has less to do with all things being equal than what has the most weight.

Having a desire without the daily discipline to achieve it makes the desire just a dream. Start walking out your dreams today.

There's no reward in quitting! Though the process is difficult, enduring to the end is its own reward.

Success is reflective to those who can recognize it. Champions always find a way!

Integrity may not be a gift, but it definitely impacts how one uses his gift.

Adversity is the proving ground for success.

Keep your HEAD UP! You can see farther.

When you are afraid to be uncomfortable, you are afraid to be successful.

Money is an object for potential, not an objective of destiny.

Avoid whistling past the "little" things and trying to get to the "big" things. Often, it's the "little" things that make the "big" things move.

Even with your eyes closed, light will wake up darkness.

Fear can be the mental prison of progress. Face it today. Your future is counting on you.

A stage doesn't determine your effort; your effort will open up a stage.

Belief in your vision needs no explanation, while success is its own revenge.

Worry is doubt masked in anxiety.

Failure is not the lack of success, but the lack of pursuit. It's OK to fail, just don't quit. Quitting gives failure a success rate.

We are faced with challenging circumstances every day. They may last for just a moment, or for a season, yet few last a lifetime.

You become what you see in yourself and not how others see you. Even an acorn knows it's an oak tree in the making. When you see yourself as valuable, then you'll know where to become relevant.

It's easy to teach something you've learned, but it's more effective to teach something you've lived.

Working with what you have prepares you for where you're going. What you have is enough for the moment. Creativity exists in the strangest surroundings.

Progress is not measured accurately in distance, but in steps. Celebrate the step you're on briefly, then take the new one.

A good name is worth its weight in gold. A good life is worth its pursuit every day. Continue to live for both.

You don't perfect being patient; however, being patient may perfect you.

———∞∞∞———

To paraphrase Joseph Addison, "If you wish success in life, make perseverance your bosom friend, experience your wise counselor, caution your elder brother and hope your guardian genius; ALL the while remembering God is your Source."

———∞∞∞———

Value does not come from validation, but through an accurate understanding of self. Discover, pursue and develop the gift called "YOU."

———∞∞∞———

Look beyond the problems of the past and pursue the promises of the future. Don't quit before you win!

———∞∞∞———

Living life to the fullest is not about how much money you're earning, but the legacy you're leaving. Set and keep the right priorities.

Identity Affirmation

I am a gift, a divine original. I was created to accomplish what no other person could at the level for which I was assigned and designed. That makes me not only special, but valuable. I see it even if others don't. I believe it even if others won't. My identity is not in what I do, but in who I am. I am fearfully and wonderfully made. I reflect the Creator. I have the ability to gain wealth. I don't die, I multiply.

The more I'm oppressed the more I progress. I am the only one who can stop my greatness. My future is bright because of my light. I AM, I BE, I SHINE!

Relational Quotes

"Therefore encourage one another and build each other up, just as in fact you are doing."

— *1 Thessalonians 5:11, NIV*

Relational Quotes

The echo of your own voice is never as sweet as the melodic harmony that the "Power of Partnership" can bring.

—————

Love is beautiful when you understand its Source and live out its intention. Don't be fooled by counterfeits, or settle for their limitations.

—————

Words are the foundation of any relationship; action is the building block that makes them visible.

—————

Making a difference is great. Being the difference is priceless!

—————

True friends do things "just because," and not simply out of convenience. Consider and celebrate your "TRUE FRIENDS" today.

—————

You never know where the twists and turns in life will take you. Don't be prideful or judgmental toward others just because your present location may be different.

—————

Putting on your "Love Shades" gives a whole new perspective to the impact you can have on others.

Lust is such a subtle deceiver of LOVE. When we study, understand, embrace and give ourselves permission to BE LOVED, lust will have no room to contaminate the true nature of a relationship.

Pursue value instead of vengeance; its success is its own vindicator.

Holding on to past hurts and pains is like carrying winter clothes on a summer vacation. You don't need them, and they can't help you. Only take with you things needed to foster growth.

When you know who you are, you can create a market or environment for being yourself. If you don't know who you are, then you become part of the environment you were created to change, and the gem inside will not be fully developed.

Learn to forgive. Forgiveness does not mean the other person is right; it just frees you to live. Start living at a 10!

I hear what you say, but I believe what you show me. It's called integrity.

There are times we become so busy trying to get our children to fit into our box that we lose sight of who they are.

Marriage is like life; you never figure it out, you just learn and grow from living it out.

The pulse of a team is based on the heartbeat of its leader.

Love sets boundaries in order to recognize its imitator: lust.

Most people would rather float the truth than deal with the reality. Truth is like your shadow; it's always there even when you don't clearly see it.

Opposites may attract; but similarities bind.

Pride can get you so focused on what you want to be that you lose sight of who you are becoming. Don't forget to check the mirror as you climb. Choose to be different.

Whatever you accept becomes true to you. Whatever you live becomes true to others, even though it may be contrary to TRUTH!

Showing your scars can help heal the wounds of many. There is power in an unedited testimony.

"Your actively engaged presence is far more valuable to a child's growth than your material presents."

Preparation is not solely about the art, but more about the person who carries the art.

Looking back gives reflection for inspection. Looking forward establishes vision for direction.

Running away from "YOU" becomes tiring to others.

Everybody wants to be attached to success; few desire to be attached to the process.

A man is not known by his age, but more for the development of his character. Make the best of being your best.

Love people and enjoy things. Don't get it twisted.

Without an accountability partner, you can think you are right. But with one, you will know what is right.

Your actively engaged presence is far more valuable to a child's growth than your material presents.

When your best isn't good enough, let *hard enough* push you toward finding *better than.* Go where you are celebrated.

The mother is the thermostat of the family; however, the father is the hand that turns the dial.

Champions look through the window when they are winning and in the mirror when losing. Those unaccustomed to winning do just the opposite.

Stay authentic in the midst of criticism and praise. People praise what they admire or appreciate; haters criticize what they don't understand or wish they possessed.

Marriage is like the cornucopia of life. It reveals, attracts, cleanses, builds, embraces and—when we are willing to pursue it—even heals. It may not be for everyone; but it's beautiful with the Right One!

Words are the least effective part of communication, but the most powerful part of Creation. Speak Life. Create Life. Live Life.

Build from your past; don't linger in it.

The background of preparation helps to establish the stage of opportunity to sustain the brightness of success.

———⊗⊗⊗⊗———

If you don't know or understand love, then power will most likely corrupt you.

———⊗⊗⊗⊗———

Good success in life is not measured by how many things you possess or how much money you have, but by how well you manage relationships.

———⊗⊗⊗⊗———

Frustration is usually the product of a lack of understanding, while patience reveals true intention.

———⊗⊗⊗⊗———

Your posterity is not solely based on how you've prospered, but also on how you've positioned your children to prosper. Create a legacy that far outlives you.

———⊗⊗⊗⊗———

Learn to love unconditionally and forgive extensively. Your peace of mind depends on it.

———⊗⊗⊗⊗———

Conditional friends are exposed in crisis. True friends will love you past "until."

Marriage is not a walk in the park. However, with a strong commitment to God, love, and a willingness to change and forgive, the walk can become more enjoyable.

—∞—

In life there are many people you care for; however, you can't care for many people. Interest vs. Responsibility.

—∞—

The quality of a relationship is best tested in times of adversity.

—∞—

The Gift of Love: "The Gift Giver gave a gift to a gift so that the gift can give it away."

—∞—

If you haven't realized how far you've come, take a look around you and see the difference in your landscape. Make each day count and each relationship purposeful.

—∞—

When you don't know who you are, you will become frustrated with whom you're with.

—∞—

Trust is not comfortable; however, it's a necessary component for growth!

—∞—

Your gift will make room for you, but it is your character that will determine how well it's furnished.

"When you don't know who you are, you will become frustrated with whom you're with."

Having confidence in who you are protects your identity in assimilation.

---⊶⊷---

The gap between IS and EXPECTATION is called FRUSTRA-TION. We close that gap by understanding that we all can err and are imperfect in some ways.

---⊶⊷---

Many promising relationships fade because, at times, we are mentally preparing ourselves more for the absence of that relationship rather than embracing its presence. This is due in part to the attachment of past hurts. We cannot fully embrace a current relationship until we let go of a former abuse.

---⊶⊷---

True networking is about building relationships before you really need them.

---⊶⊷---

When we deal with the subtle snakes in our lives during times of plenty, there will be no need for the grass to be mowed and the snakes to become more obvious.

---⊶⊷---

Legacy is determined by how you lived. History is determined by what you write and establish.

---⊶⊷---

For "US" to work together, first start by working on "U."

Your level of commitment determines the degree of your investment. Consider your return in advance.

Whoever or whatever has your thoughts has you. Take back your power.

Keep living in the positive. There is an advantage in every disadvantage. It's a matter of perspective.

Overcommunicating is a far more effective resolution tool than avoiding communication. It's not always as bad as you think. Reach out today to those you've been avoiding. You may be surprised at the results.

Wherever YOU go, YOU eventually show up! Therefore, consistently pursue healing and personal development.

We cannot afford to burn the bridge that brought us over without building one for the next generation.

Give more than you take and you'll realize that you've gained more than you've worked for.

"It is better to fail knowing you were supported than to succeed thinking you weren't."

Your purpose is in your distinctiveness and your distinctiveness is pre-wrapped in your gifts. Being different is on purpose. Celebrate it.

Without sacrifice, success is just a mirage. You are bigger than what your past has said and what your experiences have been.

Too often we're looking for people to change for us when we need to change ourselves so they can see what change looks like. Continue aiming to be a success internally and you'll find success externally.

It is better to fail knowing you were supported than to succeed thinking you weren't.

You don't realize how much you don't know because you think you know. You don't realize how much you don't do because you think you do.

Identity is what you were created to be. Ego is what you want people to think you are. Value = Identity over Ego, while Pride = Ego over Identity.

Walking in pride shortens the lifespan of success.

If you don't live what you preach and teach, then what you preach and teach becomes a speech that won't reach.

———⟨∞⟩———

The measure of a man is not in his accomplishments, nor in the trimmings that surround him. It is in the lives that his presence and influence have positively impacted.

———⟨∞⟩———

You can't be great by yourself; to achieve greatness you need others.

———⟨∞⟩———

Your ego will eventually ruin your life if you allow it to rule your life.

———⟨∞⟩———

Give your love wings and watch your life soar!

———⟨∞⟩———

Great minds think alike; extraordinary minds share their likes.

———⟨∞⟩———

Be the best YOU today and celebrate a better YOU tomorrow!

———⟨∞⟩———

A bully's strength is in your fear. When you don't fear losing, you can embrace winning; when you operate in the fear of losing, winning will continually evade you. Fight On and Fight Through!

Membership has its privileges; commitment has its advantages.

The most difficult view is in the mirror. It shows who you are and where you are at the same time. Contradicting yet confirming at the same time.

Staying in a "Victim Mentality" stunts your ability to grow. What happened to you does not define you. Move on to move up!

Feeling the need to defend yourself about something someone said can be an indicator that there is some truth in the statement. If it doesn't apply, let it fly.

Things become a lot clearer when you first look in the mirror.

If everywhere you go it smells like cabbage, it's time to check your pockets.

Although something looks the same, don't rush to treat it the same. The symptoms may be similar, but not necessarily the diagnosis. Evaluate the symptoms accurately.

Never lose yourself searching for someone else, because you will reach a place of desolation. Remember who you are each step of the way.

Don't be discouraged by the current circumstances in your house; you can still create a home. It's a matter of choice.

It's easier to call on someone you know than just someone you've met.

Adversity is the luminol that reveals true character and patience exposes deception. Nothing just happens.

Change how you think about things, and how you think about things will change.

Life is better when you take joy in doing little things for others.

Love and Respect do not automatically confer Trust.
Trust is an earned right, not an assumed privilege.

Far too many people are either stuck or comfortable with living in the "Information Age." It's time to raise the consciousness to begin moving and becoming a part of the "Application Generation." Do what you know to do.

"Change how you think about things, and how you think about things will change."

Break the silence of your past to begin a sound future. Isolation and suppression are very toxic. You are worth it.

⸺∞⸺

Reach for what first appears challenging. Release the negative thoughts. Realize it's possible. Your dream is not negotiable. Keep Striving!

⸺∞⸺

The joy of a day is sometimes measured by what you think about; the happiness of a day is oftentimes measured by who thinks about you.

⸺∞⸺

There's no right way to explain away wrong.
Integrity eventually shines through and so does deception.

⸺∞⸺

It's better to work somewhere for free than labor somewhere for less. Walk in your value!

⸺∞⸺

If you need others to recognize or acknowledge your gift, you are expecting others to invest in something you haven't exemplified in your own beliefs.

⸺∞⸺

Talent without the passion to pursue it simply dies as potential.

Too often, one desires the outcome without the process, when the outcome is the product of the process.

Obedience is the acknowledgement of knowledge, when information becomes application in your life.

The greatest gift is love; the best wrapping is the ability to influence others to positive change.

Trust is gained over time through competency and consistency.

It is better to disappoint people with the truth than to try and please them with a lie.

Good leaders can lead; great leaders can leave.

A marriage should never be defined by or lived based on the mistakes that were made, but by the love that is exhibited to God and one to another.

Trust is a key component of release.

Without Remorse, Repentance and Resolute Reversal, Reconciliation is virtually impossible to sustain.

―――⁂―――

As you share your gift with others, being of good character—the best wrapping paper—will determine its desire and the legacy you leave.

Motivation Affirmation

I choose to not be offended by those who consider me less important or make me less of a priority than others. I am who God says I am! I will go where I can be celebrated, not tolerated!

Inspirational
Quotes

"For I know the plans I have for you," declares the LORD, "plans to prosper you and not to harm you, plans to give you hope and a future."

—Jeremiah 29:11, NIV

Inspirational Quotes

Never let your view distort your vision; it is only scenery on the road called "Destiny."

—∞—

See yourself based on your calling, not your accomplishments. Your accomplishments may introduce you, but your calling promotes you.

—∞—

God works the miraculous in the midst of the incredulous; trust Him. What a Mighty God!

—∞—

Faith says, "Walk AS the road is being paved." Fear says, "How can you walk if there is no road?" If you knew the outcome every time, what would be the lesson learned?
Continue WALKING!

—∞—

Breathing is a privilege; living is a choice. Living on purpose destroys the apathy of just existing.

—∞—

It is not what a man sees before him that gives him power, but what he sees within.

—∞—

Don't reinvent the wheel, just shine it up and add new tires.

May the joys of life find and caress you as the blessings of God inspire you.

—∞∞∞—

A truth for YOU is not necessarily a truth for everyone else. That is what revelation knowledge is all about. What God has designed for you to do is not necessarily what He wants others to do. Know God for yourself to know the truth regarding your purpose.

—∞∞∞—

Celebrate your progress. You may not be where you desire, but just stop and smell the flowers that bloomed from the growth of yesterday.

—∞∞∞—

Being steeped in adversity can cause your greatness to come forth. Learn to endure. Your location is not your destination.

—∞∞∞—

If you feel like you've stalled in an area of your life, hit the "RE-FRESH" button. Stagnation can only exist if you believe you can never restart or continue.

—∞∞∞—

In life, purpose becomes the windshield of the inspired. However, comfortability can be the couch of the unmotivated. You were created for more.

—∞∞∞—

Update your address! It is time to move from living on the outskirts called "Good," when the city of "Greatness" is awaiting you.

Today is the day, now is the moment and the movement. The time is now for each of us to be in the moment and the movement of our own life. Take charge NOW!

God places some people in your life so you can GIVE; others He places so you can LIVE. The right connection in the right season is priceless.

Activity produces process while productivity yields growth. Where are you today?

Bending your knees in prayer gives you much more strength to move what is in your way than bending your arms.

Every day that you inhale and exhale is another opportunity for you to excel.

Take time out of your day to release and breathe "stress-free" air. It lets the challenges you face know you refuse to be shaken.

When you have vision, you don't settle for the transition. It does get better. Just learn in the process and keep believing.

"Keep growing like a tree, and your leaves will provide the shade needed for your legacy."

Your purpose may require a period of isolation, and may even contain seasons of insignificance. Stay focused on your assignment without wavering. Your time of unveiling is closer than you feel.

Walk confidently in the gifts and talents God has placed inside you. Do not be intimidated by those who appear to be more qualified, experienced or skilled. Remember, David used a stone and a sling to defeat a giant who appeared more qualified, experienced, and skilled.

Great moments are around you every day. Average people miss them; extraordinary people see, celebrate and embrace them. Continue to maximize each moment and be extraordinary!

Keep growing like a tree, and your leaves will provide the shade needed for your legacy.

The gifts of God are without repentance. How one chooses to use their gift is based on integrity of character.

When you awaken and agree to your giftings, you give God permission to open your eyes to opportunities to utilize them and serve others.

Stretch to reach your goals, even if you have to get on your "tippy toes."

Education plus Activation give you the Authorization of Inspiration.

———❦———

Don't pray just because there is a crisis; pray because there is a Christ. Prayer orders your day.

———❦———

A grade is simply someone else's evaluation of your best. Win by being your best everyday regardless of what others think.

———❦———

It's good to name it and claim it, but it's better to believe it and receive it. It's good to possess it, but it's better to occupy it. It's all a matter of your perspective and mental fortitude.

———❦———

Your wealthiest place is within you. When one measures their wealth by what they materially possess, they're living in spiritual poverty. Walk first in your spiritual wealth and you'll never be bankrupt.

———❦———

Just because you're expendable doesn't mean you're not valuable. Keep believing in your gift.

———❦———

Praise delivers! Complaining delays!

———❦———

Keep building your gift, regardless of who values it today. It's the small groups that prepare you for the large arenas.

When you beat your personal record, you've already won! Improvement is the soil where success grows.

If "pride goes before destruction and a haughty spirit before a fall," then value goes before construction and humility before exaltation.

Focusing on your view makes you fearful. Focusing on your vision makes you faithful.

God is always with you. When you don't feel His presence, He's most likely working to bring out the good gift He placed in you.

If you continue to focus on what you have to do, it's easy to lose appreciation for what you have already done. Praise progress regardless of the distance of accomplishment.

Whatever mountain you're facing in this season of your life you are more than able to conquer. You must believe you already possess the tools for victory. You are a champion. Champions talk to their mountains about their God; others just talk about their mountains.

Opportunity is a gift from God; preparation is faith in action; and success is the culmination of both.

If you aim for perfection, you will constantly be frustrated. Aim for excellence instead, and progress each day. It's in celebrating those small steps of progression that you find joy in the journey.

—∞∞—

Focus on your vision and spend less time rehearsing your past accomplishments. Holding on to your history only stagnates your future.

—∞∞—

The pain of pregnancy labor does not negate the process or the promise. Keep pushing!

—∞∞—

This is the year to discontinue testing the waters; it's now time to CREATE THE WAVE! Push past the fear to embrace the change.

—∞∞—

Being still doesn't mean you don't move; it simply means you move in a way that you have heard God. A seed has to die before the tree inside can come forth. That's preparation in the waiting process. Rough at times, but worth the reward.

—∞∞—

Raise your intellect by what you read. Raise your understanding by who and what you give first priority.

—∞∞—

Sometimes God allows you to get so low, to get you solo, so that you can grow.

"Being still doesn't mean you don't move; it simply means you move in a way that you have heard God."

Faith never complains about what it sees; instead it proclaims where it's going.

———◦◦◦◦———

When you are ready for God to move in your life, He will either change your environment or change the environment. Either He will change the people around you, or He will change you from being around those people.

———◦◦◦◦———

When you walk in the authority of God, people with money and power begin to fear you and become powerless against you. Favor has its benefits.

———◦◦◦◦———

Faith is the product of imagination—that God-given ability to see that with Him YOU CAN!

———◦◦◦◦———

Trust is the foundation of faith; faith is the foundation of hope; and hope is the foundation for the drive that keeps you going until opportunity is realized. As you continue to trust God for Who He is, believe that what He has said over your life will be fulfilled. You will develop the drive to Actively Anticipate as you Proactively Prepare.

———◦◦◦◦———

YOU were born with potential and value. Another year doesn't give it to you; neither will another job. They just give you the opportunity to recognize, find, appreciate and develop it. Ignore the critics who say otherwise, and press past your current view that looks contrary. Make the commitment, not a resolution, to tap into your God-given resource to produce the maximum you every day.

God can do ANYTHING, but He will not do EVERYTHING. We must be an active participant in our success.

⸺∞⸺

"A rock and a hard place" can sometime serve as the catalyst that manifests the greatness that lies within each of us. When we choose to believe in, recognize and appreciate our God-given gifts, talents and abilities, "a rock and a hard place" becomes just another platform for their expression.

⸺∞⸺

The "Midas Touch" is learning how to consistently hear and discern what opportunities God desires for you to pursue. That's when the results truly become golden.

⸺∞⸺

The question is not "What are we doing?" but rather "Who are we becoming?"

⸺∞⸺

Sight without insight ends up being blindness. Revelation is sight with insight in operation.

⸺∞⸺

Pride says, "Look at me." Humility says, "Look away from me."

⸺∞⸺

A road paved with good intentions oftentimes intersects the avenue of disappointment.

"Although God-ideas can at first seem challenging, the rewards will make the challenges laughable."

To say the word, "can't" one has to go past the word "can." Why not believe the first part and leave the rest to the doubters. It's through believing that you can and preparing like you will that you ultimately achieve your goal.

Although God-ideas can at first seem challenging, the rewards will make the challenges laughable.

Process before you progress. Make sure each decision and choice you make is worth it.

Fear is the sound of an enemy. Recognize it and act accordingly. Be thankful for the purpose of the process instead of wallowing in the pain of it.

Before, faith took a back seat to my talents and abilities. But now, my talents and abilities have taken a back seat to my faith. Proper priorities propel promotion.

PURSUE! PRESS! PERSEVERE! Your victory ultimately comes by way of your FAITH. Believe you will WIN and ACT on it. Winning is in the finishing. Keep your victory in view.

Many people have the theology; however, they haven't truly embraced the revelation of theology to be applicable in their lives. Let's be the message we know.

You may be able to exist without prayer, but you can never live without it.

—⊗⊗⊗—

Have peace in what you release and you will have power in what you pursue!

—⊗⊗⊗—

Training to be something you've never seen is the mindset of a champion. Why keep looking for the Type when you can be the Prototype!

—⊗⊗⊗—

Doubters say, "I think I can." Believers say, "I know I can." But Achievers say, "I can!" Move from thinking and believing. Avoid settling for less than your best. Your dreams are not negotiable.

—⊗⊗⊗—

When faced with a challenge in life, if there is nothing you can do to change it, just pray and don't worry. Your life has too much purpose to let a brief snapshot slow its progress.

—⊗⊗⊗—

Living by principles avoids the need for frequent divine intervention. Living by those same principles positions you for a miracle when opposition arises. Hold fast to the principles you've established and watch miracles start to happen.

—⊗⊗⊗—

Motivation is the kindling that starts the fire, but discipline is the wood that keeps the flame going.

"Have peace in what you release and you will have power in what you pursue!"

A crisis can be the thing that introduces you to the person you were called to be. Don't curse your crisis.

When you realize YOUR best is all you can give, the term competition no longer has relevance in your life. YOUR BEST may not be THE BEST, but it allows you to WIN every time. Don't compete, WIN!

Adversity gives us the opportunity to prove what we've learned in better times.

Working with what you have prepares you for where you're going. What you have is enough for the moment. Creativity exists in the strangest surroundings.

Faith says, "I would rather be in the dark trusting God, than in the light and relying on man." Don't give in. Believe!

Just when you feel all is gloomy, God shows you a rainbow.

Find time and reasons to celebrate; misery never schedules appointments.

Cogitation Affirmation:

I have become the sum total of all my thoughts; therefore, I choose to focus my thoughts on things that make me better—not ignoring challenges, but limiting their mental impact. My mind is too valuable to fill with things of lesser value. I have too much purpose attached to me to allow my mind to become engaged in what's not happening. Today, I choose to train my thoughts and discipline my mind to reach one level above yesterday.

Food for Thought

"The thorns of a rose are God's way of reminding us through nature to handle His beauties with care."

Food for Thought

The Miracle of a Gift

We have nothing to do with receiving it, but are fully responsible for how we serve it.

The 4 levels of Focus: The Candle, Light Bulb, Spotlight and Laser.

- The Candle—sheds little light on what you can see in order for you to discern the best alternative.
- The Light Bulb—gives more light to what you can see, which opens up more options.
- The Spotlight—gives light specifically to what and where you look, and puts everything else in the shadows.
- The Laser—gives a detailed, isolated narrow light that allows you to cut through all distractions and peripheral matters to focus on the priority.

Lesson From a Rose

The thorns of a rose are God's way of reminding us through nature to handle His beauties with care.

Meditating on past disappointments opens the door to doubt, which gives way to unbelief. Remember, disappointment (which is the other side of expectation) is part of life; however, discouragement is a choice. Keep believing!

It's interesting how, in society, we are more trusting of people we know little about to care for our children than we are with those we know a lot about with our things. Where do our priorities really lie?

⸻

If you want to feel wealthy, just look around and count all the things you have that you can't put a price on. It is in that reflection that you can truly appreciate life.

⸻

Be cautious of those who are willing to take the ride but unwilling to take the risk. Who are your partners?

⸻

What if everyone who graduated college found a job? What if everyone who found a job was passionate about their job? What if everyone who had passion was willing to follow that passion? Then, success would be common. Success is the result of uncommon people who dare to dream, identify a passion, follow their efforts, push pass failures, and believe and invest in themselves—regardless of preconceived limitations—to one day leave a legacy.

⸻

Knowing when to speak is as golden as knowing what to say. Every opportunity for your opinion is not always an opportunity for you to share it. Timing is the sequential part of speech that gets the maximum results.

⸻

A Chinese proverb says, "Better to light one small candle than to curse the darkness." Make the choice each day to effect change rather than be among the many that criticize it.

Walter Winchell once said, "A real friend is one who walks in when the rest of the world walks out." Evaluate your relationships to determine who your "REAL" friends are.

It has been said that when your misery factor outweighs your fear factor, change will occur. Counseling and coaching only work when your desire is for things to get better.

Did you inhale and exhale today? If so, you are already having a Great Day! Celebrate the major, yet sometimes overlooked, MIRACLES in our lives.

In a society that often magnifies the trivial and promotes ignorance, take the time to celebrate intelligence. Recognize and applaud the brilliance of others, as well as your own intelligence. You are different for a reason. Therefore, because you "stand out," go ahead and step out! It's OK...really!

Why is it that we find it so easy to say what is going wrong with us, but have difficulty stating what's going right with us? Recognize and appreciate your value. Do it today!

From a technological standpoint, your IP (Internet Protocol) address is how you are located on the worldwide web. Without an IP address, you basically cannot be found. In life you also have an IP address. It's called your Identity and Purpose. Knowing your IP gives direction to your life and allows others to see who you are and where you're going.

"Understanding is not a pre-requisite for obedience, but trust is. Have you checked your trust level lately?"

Beware of the impact of your decisions and choices. Your thinking processes determine your decisions; however, the ultimate impact of your actions is based upon your choices, which have a greater impact on your life than just making a decision.

⁓

Instead of desiring for life to be easy, why not ask God to give you the strength to endure? If you can truly focus on and tap into your inner strength, your weaknesses will die for lack of nutrition.

⁓

When was the last time you celebrated family history? We seem to have forgotten to pass on family stories of the past to inspire, inform, caution and teach our posterity. Ignorance does not change the future, but oftentimes repeats the past. Disclose, celebrate and release history! Do it today! Do it often!

⁓

When it comes to giving, some would much rather receive. Think about it…a little generosity can go a long way. However, loneliness can be a selfish person's companion.

⁓

Is it me or are we becoming less and less of a thinking society? Is common sense becoming more and more uncommon? As Tye Tribbett puts it, "Just because I feel it doesn't mean I have to fulfill it." Choose to consider your decisions before making choices.

⁓

Understanding is not a prerequisite for obedience, but trust is. Have you checked your trust level lately?

Here is a paradigm shift: Pain is good; it shows you where there is a problem. Do not try to reduce the pain until you find the problem.

Why does it seem our parents could take care of us, yet when they grow older we cannot take care of them? How are we honoring those who have invested in us?

Love is to lust what empowering is to enabling. Love GIVES of its time, self, and talents. Empowering GIVES the opportunity to think, do and achieve. Lust TAKES FROM, based on what it can get. Enabling TAKES the opportunity FROM someone to be able to get, learn, and grow. What have you been doing?

If you're not really ready for the answer, don't ask the question.

Do you spend more time watching others Tell-A-Vision than pursuing YOUR vision? Value and purpose are the drivers of life. Your life has more value than you may think. You were created with purpose on purpose. Take time today to prioritize YOUR life.

Live today without fear of failing, fear of ridicule, fear of incompetence. As Oscar Wilde once said: "Experience is simply the name we give our mistakes."

Do you look back on a task completed and think you did it well (with excellence), or just that you did it? Do your best no matter the task. That type of character often gets noticed and promoted.

———⠀⠀⠀———

There is a reason going uphill takes longer than going down-hill. Could it be that nature gives us an opportunity to think, pro-cess and weigh our movements, words and strategy? Utilize the blessings going uphill give you, because the speed of the descent often doesn't allow that chance. Live on the way up so you can shine the rest of the way.

———⠀⠀⠀———

Keep having the courage to build your dreams, regardless of the opposition or negativity you may face. As Winston Churchill put it, "Courage is going from failure to failure without losing enthusiasm."

———⠀⠀⠀———

Remain Peace-Full: Making decisions while in a state of anxiety or frustration can be detrimental and counterproductive to YOUR purpose.

———⠀⠀⠀———

Ralph Waldo Emerson once said, "The glory of friendship is not the outstretched hand, nor the kindly smile, nor the joy of com-panionship; it is the spiritual inspiration that comes to one when he discovers that someone else believes in him and is willing to trust him with his friendship." Who are your TRUE friends?

———⠀⠀⠀———

There is a difference between true and truth. Something that is true is based on the information one receives. Truth, however, is and remains, regardless of the information one possesses.

Make today an "I" day:, I am special, I am a winner, I am productive, I can do it, and I will be the best I can be. As Eleanor Roosevelt once said, "No one can make you feel inferior without your consent."

———&———

It is said that "a smile is a light in the window of the soul indicating that the heart is at home." Remind your face that your heart is at home today.

———&———

As you walk into your future, release the hurts of your past so they don't impact the actions of the present. Then, you will find fulfillment and happiness in all you do because, as Abraham Lincoln once said, "In the end it's not the years in your life that count. It's the life in your years."

———&———

Worrying and foreboding can cause you to lose sight of the moment. Set your principles and focus on your priorities and do all YOU can control. Enjoy the delightful treats that the moment of now brings, and watch the results!

———&———

Stay focused on finding, achieving and fulfilling your purpose. Don't let the vicissitudes of life knock you off course. As Stephen Covey once said, "We are not human beings on a spiritual journey. We are spiritual beings on a human journey."

———&———

What you physically see is the past. Your ability to imagine and have vision is the future in pictures. Mark Twain said, "You cannot depend on your eyes when your imagination is out of focus." Keep envisioning your dreams as if they have already happened. That way, when you arrive, success will not catch you by surprise.

"It is said that 'a smile is a light in the window of the soul indicating that the heart is at home.' Remind your face that your heart is at home today."

Getting even may make you feel good for the moment, and even enlarge who you want others to think you are. That is common. However, true strength is exhibited more by what you have the power to do with restraint than by what you physically do. Meekness is not weakness. Continue to show strength and remember, "Vengeance is mine, saith the Lord" (Romans 12:19). The battle is not yours to fight physically; it's yours to endure so that His fight gets you the win.

———

Perseverance is the product of faith (James 1:3). Someone once said, "Say what you heard until you see what you said." Be encouraged; your night season will turn around. Believe it!

———

Sometimes it takes a crisis to compel the creativity and courage within to come into view. The crisis you face just may be your "diamond" moment.

———

In life you never have to chase the things you can attract. That thought alone should give you a different perspective on the "what and why" you find yourself chasing. What are you chasing in your life: Is it money, companionship, possessions? Continue building you and developing your gifts, and you'll be amazed at what you attract that you thought you once had to chase.

———

Life has a way of taking your focus off your purpose. Avoid letting life get in the way of your vision. Take control of life. Smile often and worry less. It's a way of letting life know that you will not be defeated. Challenging? Yes. Possible? For sure. Try it today!

Prepare your character as you prepare your future. Your character has to keep up with your success for you to remain successful. Integrity trumps dishonesty—any day.

———∞———

Procrastination is the enemy of progress. Henry Kissinger once said, "Whatever must happen ultimately should happen immediately." This is your wake-up call to avoid delaying things in your life that you need to change, but you may not have the heart to adjust. Realize that this life isn't permanent, and every day is precious—too precious to stay stuck in a rut.

———∞———

If you find yourself frequently harping on the things you've done (good or bad), you are feeding your past instead of pursuing your future. Avoid getting caught staring at a mile marker of life. You have the power to pursue much more. Walk in it today. A generation is counting on you.

———∞———

Avoid taking life too seriously. Learn to laugh and de-stress. If you cannot do anything to change the outcome of a situation, then you've done enough. Julia Roberts once said, "Show me a person who doesn't like to laugh and I'll show you a person with a toe tag." Laughter is the energy boost that makes life exciting.

———∞———

Are you choosing charisma over character, show over substance, or knowledge over authority? If so, it's time for a paradigm shift. Reevaluate your priorities and watch your life change from the inside out.

"There's a big difference between quitting and releasing. When you release something, you are freely giving it up based on divine permission. Quitting implies the avoidance of a challenge."

Celebrate the seemingly minor achievements you've made so far. It is in celebrating what seems like minor accomplishments daily that makes the bigger accomplishments attainable and visible. Remember, without the hinges the door cannot be opened. Applaud yourself for the "hinges" you've placed and refined in your life and watch how many doors start to open for you.

The Process of Effectiveness: Knowledge + Wisdom + Understanding

- **Knowledge** is organized information. It gives you "What" to do.

- **Wisdom** is knowledge rightly executed. It gives you the "When" and "How" to do a thing—the most important step.

- **Understanding** is the discernment or comprehension of knowledge. It gives you the "Why" you are doing a thing. It must be parallel to **Wisdom.**

When mixed together, the success of effectiveness is achieved!

There's a difference between *quitting* and *releasing.* When you release something, you freely give it up based on divine permission. Quitting implies the avoidance of a challenge.

It's amazing how many people would rather go to a job they hate for years, than take the risk and explore the possibilities that ownership of their gift can create. Do what you are created and gifted to BE. It's the industry inside that will feed your posterity.

Doing a lot more doesn't mean you're getting a lot more done. Walking in place is good if you're exercising, but is counterproductive if you're trying to get somewhere.

———∞———

There is enough success, wealth and greatness in this earth for everyone. There is no need to criticize, minimize or hate the level of success or exposure that others get.

———∞———

Avoid getting pulled into or caught in the competitive and comparative web.

———∞———

When you can celebrate the rise of your neighbor's star, it will make yours shine that much brighter. Success is not in limited supply. However, we can limit our success when we focus on competing versus creating and co-creating.

———∞———

God gives us free will, but free will doesn't mean freedom! Free will is a gift, freedom is a choice.

———∞———

Work hard in silence and let your actions become your noise. It is then that you will see your gift making room for you.
Isn't it interesting how you still end up passing drivers who aren't kind enough to let you over? So it is in life…Keep driving and you will see how far you've gone past those who tried to delay your arrival.

"God gives us free will, but free will doesn't mean freedom! Free will is a gift, freedom is a choice."

What is **F.R.I.**–Day? A day for *Finishing, Reflecting* and *Inspecting.*

- **F**inish and tie up those loose items within your power that were left incomplete.

- **R**eflect on what you've accomplished this week based on your weekly plan.

- **I**nspect what you've expected to make sure that it met the standard you desired.

Now celebrate and applaud yourself for making your week truly productive. As you can see, Friday is not just the end of the week, but the last opportunity for you to complete, contemplate, canvass and then celebrate its ending.

Al-cronyms

> *"A HERO sees the victory at the top of the mountain over the challenge of the climb."*

Al-cronyms

L.I.V.E.
(Let Inspiration Visit Everyday)

When you **LIVE,** life takes on new meaning.

W.O.R.K.
(Wonderful Opportunity to Represent the King)

Your **WORK** will take the toil out of anything you do.

H.E.R.O.
(Heart to Engage Regardless of Obstacles)

A **HERO** sees the victory at the top of the mountain over the challenge of the climb.

P.U.N.K.
(Person Under Negative Knowledge)

The words of others should never **PUNK** you into believing something you're not.

G.U.R.U.
(God's Unlimited Resource Unleashed)

A **GURU** understands his sweet spot is attractive to others.

B.A.G.S.
(Beliefs About Gone Seasons)

Carrying **BAGS** can be detrimental to the longevity of new opportunities.

G.A.M.E.
(God's Authorized Manifested Expectation)

Keep your head in the **GAME** and enjoy the results.

P.I.E.
(Passion, Intensity and Effort)

The **PIE** approach in any activity can separate the sensational from the satisfactory.

A.I.R.
(Appreciation, Inspiration and Recognition)

Everyone needs **AIR** to help them achieve purpose.

P.I.M.P.
(Person Intentionally Manipulating Purpose)

Happiness to a **PIMP** has a short shelf life. They will eventually lose the relationships they try to control.

*"The PIE approach in
any activity can separate
the sensational from the
satisfactory."*

"Having acute discernment will avoid carrying a TOTE bag that impedes the plan for your life."

C.R.A.P.
(Continual Recurring Abundance of Problems)

Continual spiritual and personal development gives an eviction notice to the **CRAP** that tries to rent space in your life.

L.I.G.H.T.
(Leader Igniting God's Hidden Treasure)

Be the **LIGHT** that others need to see.

H.O.M.E.
(Haven Of Manifested Expectation)

Building a **HOME** takes personal investment.

T.I.M.E.
(Taking Inspection to Manifest Expectation)

In **TIME** you will know what's important for you to progress.

T.O.T.E.
(Trick Of The Enemy)

Having acute discernment will avoid carrying a **TOTE** bag that impedes the plan for your life.

C.L.U.B.
(Connection, Love, Understanding and Belonging)

People join and stay where they feel they are a part of the **CLUB.**

F.L.O.W.
(Freely Love Others Well)

When you **FLOW,** you allow life to return the nutrients needed for sustenance.

L.O.V.E.
(Learning Oneself; Valuing Everyone)

LOVE is the current that brings a smile, warms a heart and gives life FLOW.

F.U.L.F.I.L.L.
(Forge Until Life Forms Into a Living Legacy)

Make sure your goals and plans allow you to FULFILL your purpose and life mission.

M.E.N.U.
(Mentally Engaging Notes Unveiled)

The **MENU** that we entertain will eventually become the dish we eat from.

*"LOVE is the current
that brings a smile, warms a
heart and gives life FLOW."*

"When we look into the mirror and recognize our need to change, BLAME then has no soil in which to grow."

D.R.E.A.M.
(A Desire to Realize an Expected and Anticipated Manifestation)

Effort is the foot that carries your passion so that your **DREAM** can one day be manifested.

P.O.W.E.R.
(Passion to Overcome While Engaging Risk)

Utilize the **POWER** within to keep pressing on.

B.L.A.M.E.
(Becoming Less Accountable to Mature in Excellence)

When we look into the mirror and recognize our need to change, **BLAME** then has no soil in which to grow.

L.I.F.E.
(Living In Full Expression)

LIFE creates a freedom all should experience.

L.I.F.E. (Grades)

A – You **A**pplied the belief that YOU CAN to the maximum capacity.

B – You **B**elieve that YOU CAN achieve.

C – You **C**ame wondering if you were average.

D – You **D**idn't apply yourself appropriately to your potential.

F – You **F**ailed to apply the minimum requirements and stayed there.

What grade will your daily posture and pursuit produce?

Y.E.S.
(**Y**ou **E**ndeavor **S**uccess)

Whatever you say **YES** to gives it access to grow.

O.A.R.
(**O**verseer, **A**ccountability, and **R**esponsibility)

A father is an **O.A.R.** of his boat (family, domain, household).

P.I.C.
(**P**lan, **I**nitiative, and **C**onsistency)

Having a **P.I.C.** in your day can develop growth and achieve success in any area.

P.D.F.
(Purpose, Design, and Function)
The true **P.D.F.** of a thing is defined by its creator.

—∞∞—

A.I.M.
(Awareness, Implementation, and Measurement)

Awareness—Create a plan of awareness for what you desire to market, serve, or produce.
Implementation—Design a plan to effectively implement the idea, message, product, or service.
Measurement—Define the strategy and methodology to measure the success or what the "win" looks like.

Fine-tuning your **A.I.M** can greatly increase your chances of hitting the bull's-eye.

—∞∞—

T.G.I.A.
(Thank God I'm Alive)

It's great to celebrate a particular day. Yet, the fact that we get to open our eyes each day to receive 86,400 seconds (24 hours) of opportunity gives us reasons to cherish the gift God gives called, "the Present."

Notes

Notes

Notes

Notes

Notes

www.ingramcontent.com/pod-product-compliance
Lightning Source LLC
LaVergne TN
LVHW051250080426
835513LV00016B/1850